The Power of GIFT GIVING

Robert Strand

Evergreen PRESS

The Power of Gift Giving
by Robert Strand
Copyright ©2001 Robert Strand

ISBN 1-58169-055-X
For Worldwide Distribution
Printed in Canada.

Evergreen Press
P.O. Box 91011 • Mobile, AL 36691
800-367-8203

TABLE OF CONTENTS

INTRODUCTION

The happiest people I know are the people who have learned the joy of giving! Do you want to discover true joy? Do you want your life to be used in a powerful way to bless others as well as yourself? Would you like to make a difference, a *real* difference, in people's lives? Would you like to be one of those who contribute to making the world a better place?

Welcome aboard! *The Power of Gift Giving* can be your passport to a new way of living! Come along as together we explore the wonderful life-concept of giving. This book, in easily readable, bite-sized chapters that take no longer than five minutes to read, challenges you with all aspects of this way of living. It's full of human interest stories…real live people who through giving have changed their world. And as you follow them, you, too, will be enriched through the giving experience.

This is designed to be a carry-along-with-you kind of book. Stuff it into a purse or pocket and use it to fill in some of those blank spaces in your day. Take a break for your spirit.

The content has been honed over a number of years through teaching and preaching about the joy of giving. My special thanks go to those patient, wonderful people who have listened and put these truths into practice. I've been personally inspired as I've watched people give. Being a pastor has allowed me to see a slice of life not seen by most. It is my privilege to share some of those very special moments of life with you. Thanks!

My prayer is that this book will be more than reading material, that it will be a guide to a new lifestyle.

—*Robert J. Strand*

DEDICATION

This book is dedicated to my wife Donna who honed
the joy of giving into an art. She refuses to give any
gift to another that she would not like
and appreciate receiving herself.

Chapter 1

GIFTS I'D LIKE TO GIVE

The newly appointed missionary had been assigned to teach in a school in Tanzania, Africa. One of the first concepts she was attempting to impart to her students was the value of giving. She based her lessons on the lifestyle of Jesus Christ whose entire life was devoted to giving. It proved to be a new concept for her students, but she helped them understand it by using plenty of examples. And she especially emphasized the importance of generosity, the idea of sacrifice, and the value of the recipient. Following this teaching section, there was a long weekend break from school.

On the second day of the break, there was a knock on the door of the missionary's house. As she opened it, there stood one of her students, with his clothing wet with sweat from the intense African heat. He shyly handed her a beautiful seashell. She exclaimed how beautiful it was, knowing full well it must have come from quite a distance since their village was located far from the ocean.

He said, "This is for you, my teacher, in thanks for your teaching."

Thinking of the cost involved and knowing his poverty, she asked him, "Where did you get this?"

He said, "From the ocean. I picked it for you myself."

Astonished, she replied, "What a long walk that was!"

He brightened, smiled, and said, "Long walk is a part of the gift."

This student learned his lesson well. What a powerful impact that kind of gift has on the receiver!

That's what we'll be talking about in this book: THE POWER OF GIFT GIVING!

One of the most powerful biblical settings for our subject is taken from the life of Peter and John, disciples of Jesus, who went up to the temple at three in the afternoon. They were met by a beggar, a man crippled from birth, who asked for money. I love their reply: Peter said, "Silver or gold I do not have, but what I have I give you!" (Acts 3:6) What a wonderful line to live by: "What I have I give you!"

A number of years ago, as I worked my way through college, I had a job in downtown Minneapolis near the busiest pedestrian corner in the city. It was the Christmas season, and the city was filled with shoppers who all seemed to be in a rush. As I waited for the light to change, I heard the tap, tap, tap of a steel-tipped cane heading toward me. The light changed and people surged around each other to cross the street. The rhythm of the cane changed and as I looked back, I sensed that the young blind man had become confused. I offered my arm and asked where he wanted to go. The young man thanked me as I took him to the corner where he could catch his bus. He told me he had been Christmas shopping by himself for some special people. What courage!

After I left him—I still remember the feeling I had—I wished with all my heart I could have given that young man his sight. I wanted him to see the colors of the festive season, to look into the faces of others, to see the sunshine glistening on the newly fallen snow, to look into the wonderfully decorated store windows. I couldn't give him his sight—that gift is beyond me—but I thought about what I had been able to give: a few moments of care, an arm of concern, a smile in my voice, and a bit of help.

As I look back on that moment, I've often thought about other gifts I'd like to be able to give. I'd like to give a boy's daddy back to him, return a widow's beloved husband, remove the braces from the little legs of every crippled child, give virtue back to girls who have soiled themselves, take away the bars of imprisonment from men who have no hope, give hearing to the deaf and sight to the blind. These and many more are some of the gifts I'd like to give, but I don't have it in my power to do so.

But I will give what I can. I can give courage, love, hope, consideration, respect, and a bit of time! This is truly a wonderful line: "What I have I give you!" You know, when we stop to think about it, all of us have a lot to give! You do and so do I! It's not about giving what's impossible to give…it's about giving what we have to give.

The larger question is: Will we do it? Peter and John didn't hesitate!

(Acts 3:6)

⚡ POWER POINT: Every day this week see if you can help someone in need—in a small or big way, it doesn't matter.

Chapter 2
ALL I HAD TO GIVE

In Cornwall, New York, the story of a teacher and her student, who have now passed to their eternal reward, unfolded more than 100 years ago. Miss Frances Irene Hungerford, the new 8th grade teacher, was a tiny mite of a woman but warmhearted and outgoing. This small community soon learned that she was a dedicated teacher. In addition, she was a faithful church attendee, never missing a service except in an emergency.

She began the first day of school by writing the following quote on the blackboard: "Seest thou the man who is diligent in his business? He shall stand before kings" (Proverbs 22:29 KJV). Her pupils sat at their desks giggling—what person from Cornwall could possibly stand before a king?

One of her students was Steven Pigott, a tall lanky boy who was excellent at his studies. His father Pat was an Irish immigrant who could neither read nor write and who couldn't understand why Steve was so interested in books.

5

Later, Miss Hungerford asked Steve what he wanted to be. Without hesitation he answered, "A marine engineer." She assured him that he could indeed become one and encouraged him to go to college.

He entered Columbia University and worked his way through, graduating in 1903 with high honors. His former teacher sent him a telegram which simply said: "I told you so!"

Five years later, he went to Scotland and was persuaded to remain. During the following years, he played a large part in building such ships as the *Mauretania* and the *Lusitania*. Later he designed the machinery for British battleships, cruisers, and submarines. Because of his great talent and accomplishments, he was knighted by the British government and became known the world over as Sir Steven Pigott, the brilliant marine engineer.

With all his honors, he never forgot the humble little teacher who had been his encouragement. She was honored at a very special 85th birthday party when many of her students, including Sir Steven, came home to celebrate with her. Quite a large percentage of her students had gone on to have wonderful careers, but Steven was the most famous of them all. She was asked by a reporter about the secret which allowed her to be so influential in so many young lives. She said, without hesitation: "You see, all I had was love."

We, too, can give love! It's just hard to do if your own life is devoid of love. In the same way, you can't spread sunshine if there isn't joy in your own life. You can't share faith if you are lost. You can't impart courage if your life is filled with fear. And you can't warm others with love if your own spirit is shriveled up and selfish. Perhaps this is a good point at which to stop and take a "life inventory." What do you have that you can give to others?

A surgical magazine tells of a hard-pressed, irritable, nervous, overworked emergency room surgeon in a busy New York hospital getting ready to perform an emergency operation. He was in a hurry. The patient was a beautiful 17-year-old girl who had been seriously injured in an auto accident. The doctor administering the anesthesia said kindly, "Relax, breathe deeply, and your pain will be gone."

The girl spoke up: "Would you mind if I repeated the 23rd Psalm which my mother taught me?"

The surgeon nodded, and the girl began: "The Lord is my shepherd; I shall not want…" The surgeon continued his preparations, but everyone else stood still, listening. They had heard these wonderful words in church many times but they never sounded so moving as in this operating suite.

She went on, "Though I walk through the valley of the shadow of death, I will fear no evil: for thou art with me…" The cone was about to be lowered over her face to begin the anesthesia.

"Hold it," said the surgeon, "let her finish." Then he moved over closer and spoke to his patient: "Go on, honey, say it to the end and say it for me, too, won't you?"

They all listened quietly as her heart, full of faith, filled the operating room with some of the most moving words ever written: "Thy rod and thy staff they comfort me…" The doctor looked down at her. He was relaxed, his sense of irritation and hurry was gone. There was no feeling of other duties pressing in on him. His patient was at peace and ready. Everyone in the room had been lifted by the young girl's faith. How could an operation performed under such conditions be anything but a success?

It wasn't much…but she freely gave it! What a wonderful gift of peace in a place where turmoil reigned. Peace was given, and all of the recipients were blessed. A better gift, who can find?

(Proverbs 22:29; Psalm 23)

⚡ POWER POINT: Make an inventory of everything (both material and non-material) that you have to give to others. You may be surprised!

Chapter 3
IF THAT'S ALL...

This story took place in a small, central Florida town in a home for unwanted, abused, and abandoned little boys. It was a very humble orphanage. Resources were scarce, so the furnishings were sparse but homey. The kindly matron who owned the orphanage didn't have much by way of worldly goods, but she more than made up the lack by loving the boys, mothering, and disciplining and caring for them. She also taught them how to love God, how to read their Bibles, how to pray, and how to become a person of character.

A well-to-do lady from a distant city was scheduled to arrive for the purpose of adopting one of the boys. The preliminary paperwork had been completed, and the day of the visit was at hand. There was excitement among the staff of the orphanage because one of their boys would be placed in a wonderful home. The chosen boy would soon have a successful businessman for a father and a beautifully groomed and stately lady for a mother.

Soon the woman arrived. She spent time chatting

with the matron and the lady from the placement service who was handling the adoption. She was taken on a tour of the place and had an opportunity to see all the boys. The one who was to be adopted had already been selected, and now it was time for the important interview.

They gathered in a small office: prospective mother, orphanage matron, and the representative from the placement service. Then the boy was brought into the room. Small talk was the order of the hour.

Soon the prospective mother began to question the little boy, which brought a bit of tension in the air. She asked, "Do you have a bicycle?"

"No, ma'am," he answered.

"Do you have a Nintendo®?" was her next question.

"No, ma'am, I don't."

"Do you have your own stereo?"

"No, ma'am."

"Do you have your own room?"

"No, ma'am."

"Do you have your own pair of roller blades?"

"No, ma'am."

"Do you…" she began to ask once more.

He interrupted her, "Please, ma'am, if that's all you're going to give me, I'd rather stay right here."

Pretty wise for a seven-year-old, wouldn't you agree? "If that's all…" says it all! He had already discovered a truth which has been lost on many adults. Jesus said it for all of us for all time, "…life does not consist in the abundance of his possessions!" (Luke 12:15b)

This truth is born out in our younger generation and has been confirmed by any number of surveys. Our children do not want "things" as much as they want our time. When asked what they want the most, overwhelmingly children have responded, "more time with my parents." Money cannot buy that. Material things cannot take the place of quality time together as a family.

We can expand this concept into our adult lives. Our world is becoming a lonely place. Our society has made it possible for people to "cocoon" by working with computers, shopping on the internet, communicating by e-mail, all without ever speaking to or touching another living human being. The more high tech our world is becoming, the more "high-touch" our relationships need to be!

Unfortunately we have come to the place where we now *love things and use people*. We have it backwards. We must re-learn how to *love people and use things*. The area of giving is an excellent place in which to express love for our fellow man.

Most everyone would agree in principle that the *intangible* things of life are more important than the *tangible* things. Finding time to develop and share the intangibles takes a commitment which many of us are not willing to make.

Stop and take an in-depth look at your important relationships! Would you rather give things to cover up for your guilt or lack of time or will you commit to the more serious side of a relationship?

Hear it once more, "Please, ma'am, if that's all you are going to give me, I'd rather stay here!"

(Luke 12:15b)

⚡ POWER POINT: Send an e-mail or letter to someone who has been on your mind lately. Share with them something that you appreciate about them.

Chapter 4

THE SOURCE OF GIFTS

Dwight Nelson recently told this true story about a pastor in his town. (Folks, you just can't make up stuff like this!) A kitten climbed up a tree in his backyard and then was afraid to come back down. The pastor coaxed it, offering it warm milk and other inducements to come down. But the kitty simply would not budge.

The pastor looked at the tree carefully and decided that it wasn't sturdy enough for him to climb. Thinking creatively, he decided that if he looped a rope around the upper part of the tree and tied it to his car, he could inch the car forward and bend the tree over. At that point, he figured he could probably reach up and get the kitten. He got the rope out of his garage, drove the car into the backyard, tied the rope to the tree and car and it worked—the tree began to bend over. He figured if he went just a tiny bit further, he would be able to reach the kitten easier.

But as he inched forward, the rope broke! The tree went "boooiiing!" The kitten instantly sailed through the air, out of sight. The pastor felt terrible. He looked around to see if anyone else had noticed what just happened or where the kitten had landed. No one! He walked all over the neighborhood looking for the kitten, asking people if they'd seen it. Nobody had seen a stray kitten.

So he prayed a little prayer: "Lord, I commit this kitten to Your keeping," and went about his business. A few days later, he and his wife were shopping at the grocery store and met one of his church members. He noticed cat food in her shopping cart. He was amazed because this woman was a notorious cat hater. He was curious so he asked, "Why are you buying cat food when you hate them so much?"

She replied, "You won't believe this!" She proceeded to tell them how her little girl had been begging for a cat, but she kept refusing. The child was persistent and kept on asking. Finally the mother told her little girl, "Well…if God gives you a cat, I'll let you keep it."

She continued, amazement in her voice, "I watched my girl go out into the yard, get on her knees and ask God for a cat. And really, Pastor, you won't believe this, but I saw it with my own eyes. A kitten suddenly came flying out of the blue, with its paws spread out and landed right in front of her!"[1] God does work in mysterious ways!

So where do good gifts come from? I'm glad you asked because the answer has already been penned by a man named James: "Don't be deceived…. Every good and perfect gift is from above, coming down from the Father of the heavenly lights, who does not change like shifting shadows. He chose to give us birth through the word of truth" (James 1:16-18).

Ultimately we must agree. Yes, everything that is good and perfect has its source in a loving, heavenly Father. Everything we have that can be given to others comes from above. We have to understand that we brought nothing into this world, and we can take nothing out. We are simply stewards, managing heavenly resources placed into our trust.

When we put this concept into action, it becomes an effective antidote to greed and hoarding. We have been given these things freely, and freely we should also give them to others. Generous, giving people are the kind of folks I want to have in my circle of relationships. In this world, the takers may have more of this world's earthly goods, but it is the givers who sleep better at night.

Notice how everything God has created is designed to give. Both animals and plants live to reproduce. Each animal mates and brings forth young. Each plant grows, buds, blossoms, and provides a seed so the process can go on. The seed, combined with soil, sun, nutrients, rain, and time, brings a bountiful harvest which feeds the world.

God has created a "giving" world. That's a clue to how we should live in His world. We are known by our actions. Let's be known by our giving!

Thank God for Calvary! Thank Him for eternity!

Thank Him for hope that is eternal! There is a better way!

[1] Barb Stephens, Fort Collins, Colorado, from *Parables*, *etc.*, Vol. 20, Num. 4, edited, used with permission.

(James 1:16-18a; Romans 1:20-21;
Psalm 103:1-5)

⚡ POWER POINT: Ask God to help you make out gift lists for those you love. He knows their hearts and can help you find just the right gift that will bless them.

Chapter 5

THE ABUNDANCE MIRACLE

Many people are concerned about "giving it all away." Their thinking goes something like this: "If I give too much away, I will exhaust all of my resources." We've already taken a brief look at the ultimate source of all good gifts but haven't yet taken an in-depth look at the generosity of God. Consider the following with me...

Moses was called by God to lead the children of Israel out of Egyptian bondage into the desert. But what was he going to do with them at that point? Let's consider some of the logistics the Israelites were facing. Most theologians believe that the number of people who came out of Egypt was between two and three million. They had to be fed! How would you like to be responsible for this huge dinner crowd? An anonymous Quartermaster General in the U.S. Army calculated that Moses would have needed approximately 1,500 tons of food per day to feed all of the people! Supplying the food itself would have been a problem,

17

but consider the problem of transporting that much food. He estimated it would have taken two freight trains each about a half mile long every day to accomplish the task.

There's another problem...how are you going to cook the food out in the desert? About 4,000 tons of firewood would have been needed every day. More freight trains. And don't forget, they would have needed these supplies every day for 40 years!

Oh, yes! They also needed water to survive. If each person had enough to drink and a little left over to wash the dishes and scrub their faces and hands, it would take approximately 11,000,000 gallons each day! Plan on another freight train each day just to bring the water!

There's more...have you given serious thought to crossing the Red Sea? They had to get across in a single night! If they travelled double file, the line would have been about 800 miles long and would have required 35 days and nights. There had to be a huge opening in the Red Sea at least three miles wide so they could walk 5,000 abreast to get across in a single night!

There are other logistical problems to consider. Each time they set up camp at the end of a day, they required a campground about two-thirds the size of Rhode Island! This amounted to an area about 600 to 750 square miles! Awesome!

Can you imagine what it would take to provide clothing for these millions? That's another problem that God easily solved. He saw to it that their clothes and shoes did not wear out for 40 years!

Do you think Moses had all this figured out before he led them out of Egypt? Do you think he gathered his leadership people together so they could plan strategy and supply lines and food sources? I don't think so.

How did it all happen? Simple...Moses believed in the God who had called him to leadership and trusted in God for the details. God took care of the mundane; He gave them: heating (a pillar of fire by night), cooling (a pillar of cloud by day), food from heaven (manna) that was delivered every morning around each of their tents, and clothes that didn't wear out. What a journey!

Now the question to which we have been working our way: Do you think God will have any problem taking care of all your needs *and* your giving requirements? I shared all of the above to let you see that God's resources are endless. He can supply enough both for our own journey as well as for helping others along theirs.

Here's the promise which releases resources sufficient to meet your needs as well as some of the needs of others: "And my God will meet all your needs according to his glorious riches in Christ Jesus!" (Philippians 4:19)

Can God do it? Always! Will your needs exhaust His supplies? Never!

It's sad but true—we live far beneath the possibilities available to us in Christ Jesus! There's always enough for you *and* your gift giving!

(Philippians 4:19)

POWER POINT: Look carefully at the people around you. What can you share with one of them that will ease their journey today?

Chapter 6

ON RECEIVING A GIFT

Years ago, there was a great famine in Germany after World War II. The poor were the ones who suffered most severely from hunger. In one particular small town, there was a wealthy man who was living quite comfortably. However, he was a man of compassion who committed himself to helping 20 needy families in the town. He sent for one child from each family and gathered them all together. He had a large basket filled with bread set in the middle of the room and instructed the children, "In this basket there is a loaf of bread for each of you to bring home to your family. Take one and come back every day at this same time until the famine is over. I will give you a loaf of bread every day. And often there will be other items of food here to help you survive."

The children were famished! They ran to the basket and struggled for the largest loaf possible. As soon as they each had grabbed a loaf, they ran out the door without a word of appreciation for the gracious man. When the others were gone, one little girl named

Gretchen remained. She quietly walked to the basket and removed the last loaf. It was a much smaller loaf, but Gretchen clasped it to her chest as if it were a fabulous treasure. She walked over to the kind man, looked up into his eyes, and told him how much she and her family appreciated his generosity.

The next day, all the children returned on time for their bread. They were just as rude and greedy as they had been on the preceding day. But little Gretchen just waited patiently at the back of the line until her turn came. When she reached the basket, once again there was only one tiny loaf of bread remaining. Gretchen approached her benefactor with her loaf cradled carefully in her hands and told him how wonderful he was to her and her family.

Day after day the children received the nourishing bread for their families. One day when Gretchen took the loaf of bread home, her mother cut into it and out dropped six shining silver coins.

"Oh, Gretchen," her mother exclaimed, "this must be a mistake. This money belongs to the kind gentleman. Run back to him, tell him what happened, and return his money."

Gretchen did as her mother told her, but when she handed the money to him, the wealthy man smiled and told her, "No, Gretchen, this was no mistake. I had the silver baked into the smallest loaf to reward you for your attitude of patience, humility, and gratitude."

Gretchen thanked him profusely and he replied,

"Gretchen, you and your family will be well taken care of until the famine is over. I will see to that."

What happens if you have sacrificially given a gift and the recipient doesn't acknowledge it or offer you thanks? Our first reaction might be that we would give nothing further to such a selfish, self-centered person. But is that the proper way to handle the situation? The man in our story continued to give bread to all of the 20 families as long as the famine lasted, even though he could have felt justified in cutting off the ungrateful 19 children.

What would Jesus do? Did He only give to those who were grateful for what they had received? Not really. We all remember the story of the ten lepers who were healed, but only one returned to offer thanks, and he was a member of the despised Samaritans. What happened to him? Jesus said to him, "Rise and go; your faith has made you well" (Luke 17:19). Jesus is really telling him he has become well spiritually and psychologically.

The leper who was grateful received more than the other nine, just as Gretchen's family received more than the other children's. But Jesus didn't retract his healing of the ones who showed no appreciation.

At my first pastorate, I was young and fresh out of college. One of our parishioners was Mrs. Taylor, a widow who lived on a mere pittance. Money was very scarce in her humble household. One Sunday morning after church, when I was shaking hands with the people as they left the sanctuary, she pressed a half dollar coin into my hand. Immediately I refused it by saying, "Mrs. Taylor, you can't do that. I can't take that from you."

She fixed her eyes on me, pointed a bony finger at me, drew herself up to her full 4' 11" and said, "Young man, God told me to give this to you. Now will you steal the blessing of my being obedient? Will you steal from me the joy of giving because you're too proud to accept a gift from a 79-year-old lady? You, young man, must learn how to be a grateful receiver!"

With that, I humbly replied, "Thank you for the gift and thank you for the lesson."

I've never forgotten that, and I hope that I never will.

(Luke 17:19)

POWER POINT: Think about the gifts you have recently received. What kind of thanks have you given?

Chapter 7

COSTLY GIVING

It's not particularly surprising when teens fall in and out of love for one reason or another or maybe no reason at all. Normally, teens get over these hurts and move on with life to find another significant person.

This typical pattern of teen love began as 15-year-old Felipe Garza, Jr., dated Donna Ashlock, who was a year younger. They dated until Donna cooled this puppy-love romance and began seeing other boys.

One day, Donna doubled over in intense pain. Doctors soon discovered that Donna was dying of a degenerative heart disease and desperately needed a heart transplant. Felipe heard about Donna's condition and told his mother, "I'm going to die, and I'm going to give my heart to my girlfriend." Mrs. Garza knew that teenage boys say some of the most irrational things from time to time and didn't think a lot about what he had said. After all, Felipe appeared to be in perfect health.

Three weeks later, Felipe woke up and complained of pain on the left side of his head. He became short of breath and soon couldn't even walk. He was rushed to the hospital emergency room in a state of collapse, where it was discovered that a blood vessel in his brain had burst leaving him brain dead. Felipe's sudden death shocked his doctors.

Remembering his words, his family decided to let physicians test him while he remained on a respirator, to see if his heart would be a match for Donna. When they found it was, Felipe's family gave permission for the doctors to remove his heart for her, and his other organs for those in need of transplants.

So Donna received Felipe's heart! The transplant operation was a success. Afterwards, Donna's father told her Felipe had evidently been sick for about three months before he died. He said, "He donated his kidneys and eyes…"

There was a pause, and Donna said, "And I have his heart."

Her father said, "Yes, that was what he and his parents wished."

Several days later, the funeral procession seemed to roll on forever through the orchards and fields of Patterson, California. It was so long, it might have been one for a prince, but it was for Felipe. His only claim to fame was his gift.[2]

Although Felipe's gift was special, it is truly an unforgettable human experience when a person deliberately chooses to lay down their life so that someone else can live. We read about it in stories of people who have thrown themselves between children crossing a street and a car barreling down on them. We see it in stories of people on sinking ships with only a few places left in the last lifeboat. We see it in people who have defended others against attackers—both animal and human—and died in the attempt. If you were the one who was saved, every moment you lived thereafter would be both a tribute and testimony to the one who made the supreme sacrifice.

One question comes to mind at this point: Is a gift really a gift if it doesn't cost you something to give?

On one occasion in the Old Testament, King David was to build an altar and sacrifice to the Lord. Araunah, the Jebusite, offered to give him the land and whatever was needed to make a burnt offering. But the king replied to Araunah, "No, I insist on paying you for it. I will not sacrifice to the Lord my God burnt offerings that cost me nothing!" (2 Samuel 24:24)

What a powerful statement! I will not give anything to my God that costs me nothing! What a powerful concept!

Giving is a choice. First comes the decision to give a gift, then comes the harder part. How costly will this gift be? How will it fit the occasion? None of us would dare be guilty of giving cheap gifts to royalty, would we? Of course not. We would want the gift to represent us and to represent some sort of sacrifice. What we give to God and His work on this earth or what we give to others should be measured by the same criteria. Is it really worthy to be called a gift?

The recipient may not have a clue about how

much the gift has cost you either in money or time or care. But you and God will know whether this is indeed a real gift. And when you give it, don't tell the receiver how much of a sacrifice it has been for you. Only God needs to know…and He does.

[2] Chad Miller, *The Pastor's Story File*, 7/86, Adapted, used by permission.

(II Samuel 24:24)

 POWER POINT: Have you ever considered filling out an organ donor card?

Chapter 8

JOY IN GIVING

The Rev. Earl T. Wheatley of the Parkview Church of God relates the following story:

A few years ago, our church, Parkview Church of God, saw a miracle. A tiny baby boy was born to a fine young couple in our church, Tony and Sharon Pompelia. Within minutes of his birth, doctors realized something was seriously wrong with this child. Even before his mother was able to hold him in her arms, he was rushed over 200 miles from the hospital here in Meridian to the Oschner Foundation Hospital in New Orleans. For the first six weeks of Tyler Pompelia's young life, his parents visited him in the neonatal intensive care unit of that huge medical facility.

Neither of Tyler's kidneys were performing properly. Even after leaving the hospital, their function and development were severely limited. Again and again as he grew, Tyler had to return to the hospital. Pills and needles and painful tests were a regular part of his life. Just one year ago, Tyler learned how to give himself a large, painful shot in the stomach each morning as he began his day.

A miracle has recently taken place in Tyler's life that has changed it forever. Six weeks ago Tyler received a mature, healthy donated kidney. This donor kidney came from Sharon, his mother. She gave to her son the gift of life two times…17 years apart!

The transplant procedure included grueling tests, major surgery, and a prolonged recovery in the hospital. As I talked with the family, I marveled at such love, such sacrifice. When the surgery began, mother and son were lying on gurneys beside each other.

Sharon looked over at her son and asked, "Are you scared?"

Tyler's eyes filled with tears, and he nodded, "Yes."

Sharon reached over, took his hand, and said, "Me, too."

Through all the tension and stress, Sharon never wavered. As I saw this family's courage and love, I marveled at the sacrifice being made. A healthy body was being pierced by the surgeon's knife. With a chance that surgery might not go well, there was the realistic possibility of death. As I watched Sharon's concern and fear, I also saw something else. It dawned on me…Sharon was glad to do this! She was excited about the possibilities! This was a happy, joyful act of giving![3]

What a lesson on love and sacrifice! The true gift of love is never a grudging gift or it's not a gift at all. A joyful attitude is always part of a true gift. No wonder the Bible says, "Each should give what he has decided in his heart to give, not reluctantly or under compulsion. For God loves a cheerful giver" (2 Corinthians 9:7).

With what sort of attitude do you give? Are you reluctant? Do you feel under pressure? Are you motivated by guilt? Or do you give joyfully, cheerfully, happily? And are you pleased with the privilege of giving something that makes a difference? The attitude of the giver always has an effect on the one who is on the receiving end. You can't easily hide a reluctant attitude when you're giving.

That brings us to consider another thought. Is the gift given for *your* benefit or the *receiver's* benefit? Often people give because it will benefit them, and they don't care about the person or institution receiving the gift. They just want to receive the credit for it, which makes you wonder about all those designated gifts which have plaques affixed to them in hospitals, schools, colleges, universities, and other charities. Stadiums, streets, colleges and buildings—they're all named after donors. How much would charitable giving decrease if the giver didn't receive any mention or was not given some special kind of recognition?

The bottom line to every gift is how and in what attitude it will be given. Will the real benefit be on the part of the receiver or will it benefit and bring some kind of reflected glory to the giver? Think about it.

[3]Earl T. Wheatley, *The Pastor's Story File*, Oct. 1997, Adapted, used by permission.

(2 Corinthians 9:7)

⚡ POWER POINT: Send your parents a note on your birthday (or any time, for that matter) expressing your thankfulness for the gift of life.

Chapter 9

WHY IS IT MORE BLESSED?

For giving is living, the messenger said,
Go feed the hungry love's sweet bread,
Must I keep giving again and again
My selfish and quarrelous answer ran.
Oh, no, said the angel, piercing me through
    and through.
Just give until the Master stops giving to you!
Author unknown

Paul the Apostle was quoting Jesus Christ when he told the elders at the church in Ephesus, "It is more blessed to give than to receive" (Acts 20:35b). It's interesting to note that neither Jesus nor the apostle explained the reasons behind the statement. To them it was probably obvious that we receive many blessings when we give with the correct attitude. But if you need to know some of the other reasons why, let me suggest the following:

GIVING BRINGS YOU INTO A
PARTNERSHIP WITH GOD

Who wants to partner with God? Me, and hopefully, you! This is the all-time best win-win/no-lose kind of arrangement. In the last book of the Old Testament, God asks for the opportunity to prove Himself to you. In essence, He says, "Please, allow Me to bless you. When you do your part in giving, I will do my part in blessing your giving!" (See Malachi 3:10-11.)

YOUR GIVING WILL OPEN THE
WINDOWS OF HEAVEN

When the windows of heaven are opened on your behalf, what will come flooding out? Blessings! And when God blesses, He's not stingy! He doesn't simply dribble, sprinkle, or drizzle out His blessings—they are poured out! (Again, see Malachi 3:10.)

YOUR GIVING TRIGGERS AN ENTIRELY
NEW PERSPECTIVE

Human nature is naturally stingy, selfish, and greedy. The heart that is still unregenerate is self-centered. Our world lives with the attitude, "I'm going to get mine any way that I can...sorry about you and yours." Giving initiates the exact opposite. Giving allows life to flow outward instead of just inward. The giver begins to see others and their needs and responds to them. Giving is a life-changing experience.

YOUR GIVING WILL BLESS OTHERS

Look about you and you will see a hurting world: The homeless roam our streets; the hungry rummage through garbage for some morsel; babies cry from mal-nourishment; teens run away from abusive homes; many are caught in the trap of addictions; the elderly are put out to pasture; and the needs around us go on and on. Jesus said, "I tell you the truth, whatever you did for one of the least of these brothers [or sisters] of mine, you did for me" (Matthew 25:40). James, the brother of Jesus, tells us that one of the marks of pure religion is "to look after orphans and widows in their distress…" (James 1:27a). Why are we blessed with an abundance? Simply so we can give to others.

YOUR GIVING WILL BRING
BLESSINGS TO YOU THE GIVER

There is no way to really explain this and how it happens…but when you give, you will be blessed! It may not be in monetary ways, but God has His ways of adding blessings to your life. When you really, hon-estly, truly give a gift…you cannot run fast enough to escape the blessing that will come your way. When you are obedient, you will be blessed! It's as simple as that!

YOUR ACT OF GIVING IS A WITNESS

One way to judge anyone's character is to discover whether or not they keep the promises they have made. God always keeps His word and fulfills His promises! My challenge is give God the opportunity to prove Himself to you. God says go ahead and prove Me, try it and be surprised!

One day I asked one of my parishioners, a menial laborer in the construction business, how he and his wife could give so liberally to the church. I knew his salary wasn't that great, but they were very generous people. He smiled and replied: "I just shovel it out as God shovels it in, and God just uses the biggest shovel."

God has already put his name to the contract in Malachi 3:10. Now, if you'll just sign your name beneath His, you, too, will really discover why it is more blessed to give that it is to receive!

(Acts 20:35b; Malachi 3:10-11; Matthew 25:40; James 1:27a)

POWER POINT: Ask God to help you begin to bless others because you have been blessed. Then when they attempt to thank you, tell them to "pass it on."

Chapter 10

THE RICHEST FAMILY

Here's a story you won't likely forget. It reminds us that no matter how little we have, we can be rich.

It was Easter, 1946. I was 14, my little sister Ocy was 12, and my older sister Darlene 16. We lived at home with our mother and the four of us knew what it was like to do without many things. My dad had died five years before, leaving Mom with seven kids to raise with no money. By 1946, my oldest two sisters were married, and my brothers had left home.

A month before Easter, the pastor of our church announced that a special Easter offering would be taken to help a poor family. He asked everyone to save their money in order to give sacrificially. When we got home, we talked about what we could do. We decided to buy 50 pounds of potatoes and live on them for a month. This would allow us to save $20 of our grocery money for the offering. Then we thought if we kept our electric lights turned out as much as possible and didn't listen to the radio, we'd save money on that month's electric bill. Darlene got as many house and yard cleaning jobs as possible, and both of us babysat for everyone we could. For 15¢ we could buy enough cotton loops to make three pot holders that we could sell for $1, so we invested a little of our money and made $20 on them.

That month was one of the best of our lives. Every day we counted the money to see how much we had saved. At night we'd sit in the dark and talk about how the poor family was going to enjoy having the money the church would give them. We had about 80 people in church, so we figured the offering would surely be 20 times whatever amount of money we had to give. After all, every Sunday the pastor had reminded everyone to save for the sacrificial offering.

The day before Easter, Ocy and I walked to the grocery store and got the manager to give us three crisp $20 bills and one $10 bill for all our change. We ran all the way home to show Mom and Darlene. We never had so much money before.

That night we were so excited we could hardly sleep. We didn't care that we wouldn't have any new clothes for Easter—we had $70 for the sacrificial offering. We could hardly wait to get to church!

On Sunday morning, rain was pouring down all the way to church. We didn't own an umbrella, but it didn't matter to us how wet we got. We all sat on the second row from the front, excitedly waiting for the offering to be taken.

When the offering basket was passed, Mom put in the $10 bill and each of us girls put in a $20. As we walked home after church, we sang all the way. At lunch, Mom had a surprise for us. We had boiled Easter eggs with our fried potatoes.

Late that afternoon, the minister drove up. Mom went to the door, talked with him for a moment, and slowly came back with an envelope in her hand. She opened the envelope and out fell a bunch of money. There were three crisp $20 bills, one $10 bill, and seventeen $1s.

Mom put the money back in the envelope. We didn't talk, we just sat and stared at the floor. We had gone from feeling like millionaires to feeling like poor white trash.

I knew we didn't have a lot of things other people had, but I'd never thought of us as being poor. That Easter Day I found out that the minister thought we were poor because he had brought *us* the money designated for the poor family. Therefore, we must be poor.

We sat in silence for a long time before we went to bed. Throughout the following week, we went through the motions of going to school and doing our chores at home, but no one talked much. Finally on Saturday, Mom asked us what we wanted to do with the money. What did poor people do with money? We didn't know, but now we did know that we were poor.

We didn't look forward to going to church the next day. At the service, we had a missionary speaker who talked about how churches in Africa made buildings out of sun-dried bricks. He shared how they needed money to buy roofs and that $100 would put a roof on a church. The missionary asked, "Can't we all sacrifice to help these poor people?"

We looked at each other and smiled for the first time in a week. Mom reached into her purse and pulled out the envelope. She passed it to Darlene; Darlene gave it to me; I handed it to Ocy; and Ocy put it in the offering.

When the offering was counted, the minister said it was a little over $100. The missionary was excited. He hadn't expected this from our small church. He exclaimed, "You must have some rich people in this church!"

Suddenly it struck us! We had given $87 of that "little over $100!" *We were the rich family* in our church! From that day on, I've never been poor again! I've always remembered how rich I am because I have Jesus![4]

[4]Eddie Ogan, *Mountain Movers*, June, 1993. Condensed, permission given.

(Matthew 5:3; Hebrews 13:16)

⚡ POWER POINT: Is there something you can sacrifice in order to meet the needs of someone else?

Chapter 11

THE "AVERAGE GIVER" PROFILE

Ask people their opinion on just about anything, and they will freely tell you. But ask them about their money and how they give it, and you'll likely meet with silence or hostility. Most Americans are secretive about how much they earn, what they do with their money, and how much they give away. This secretiveness could well be a cover-up for an embarrassing truth. To discover the truth, we must follow the money.

How generous are we with our money? One thing we know: Americans, when compared to any other nation on earth, are very generous.

Robert Wuthnow in his book, *God and Mammon in America*, states: "Total giving to charitable organizations of all kinds, both in absolute figures and as a proportion of income, is higher in the United States than in virtually any other advanced industrial society." (The only possible exception is Israel.)

Okay, so how generous are Americans? When we

41

compare ourselves to biblical standards, not very! The IRS reports that since 1975 Americans who itemize deductions on their tax returns have claimed that between 1.6% and 2.16% of their income went to charitable concerns. To confirm this, the American Association of Fund-Raising Counsel (AAFRC) says that giving has ranged between 1.7% and 1.95% of personal income over the past 20 years. Included in the figures are the 31% of American households who say they *give no money away*.

Over the long haul, American giving stays about the same, according to Giving USA: "Giving has represented about two percent of gross domestic product for the past four decades."

An interesting fact which shows up again and again is that there is a particular kind of person who gives generously. This same person can also be found volunteering in their community—90% of them give to charitable causes, with their households giving 2.6% of their income, quite a bit higher than the national average.

But the people who give most generously are not necessarily those who can best afford it. The "poorest" givers—those who give the lowest percentage of their income—are those who earn $40,000 to $100,000 per year. The most generous groups—those who give the highest *percentage* of their income to charity or church—are those who make less than $20,000 per year and those who make over $100,000 per year. We must understand, of course, that people will generally give more as they make more, but it's often a smaller *percentage* of their income.

Age is also a factor. The most generous donors according to Gallup polls, are those in the 35-44 and 55-64 age groups. Their proportional giving was only exceeded by those in the 75 and up age group.

According to the Barna Research Group, "The common wisdom that Baby Boomers and Baby Busters are selfish and don't give to charity is a myth."

Here's a zinger...people who attend church weekly (38% of Americans) give two-thirds of all charitable contributions in the nation! This is according to the Independent Sector Gallup Poll. Weekly church attendees give 3.4% of their income, while those who attend on Christmas and Easter average 1.4%, and those who do not attend at all give 1.1%.

Robert Wuthnow says, "Religious conservatives are more likely to make the connection between faith and money than religious moderates and liberals." He further states, "What does make a difference is believing that the Bible should be taken literally."

Dean Hoge adds, "Those who say their primary duty is to help others to commit their lives to Jesus Christ gave more than any others."

Jesus said it first: "If you want to be perfect, go, sell your possessions and give to the poor, and you will have treasure in heaven. Then come, follow me" (Matthew 19:21). And: "Where your treasure is, there your heart will be also" (Matthew 6:21).

(Matthew 19:21; 6:21)

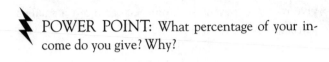 POWER POINT: What percentage of your income do you give? Why?

Chapter 12

GIVE IT BACK

Late one spring, a family of five was driving through Georgia in a Volkswagen Beetle packed with kids and luggage. It was late at night and raining so heavily they could barely see to drive. As they inched their way along, windshield wipers futilely attempting to clear the windshield, they noticed a man and woman walking along the highway in the pouring rain. They pulled over, asked if they could help, and saw that the woman carried a baby in her arms.

The woman said they lived in a town some miles back, but the electrical storm had caused a short in the wiring of their house, starting a fire which burned it to the ground, including their car parked in the attached garage. They had barely escaped with their lives and were now walking to the next town to stay with her sister and family until further help and provision could be made. Feeling sorry for the destitute family and realizing there was no way to pack three more people into the tiny VW, the father reached into his wallet and pulled out a $20 bill and gave it to the couple. The wife rummaged around and found some raincoats for them to wear. Then they drove away into the night.

A couple of miles down the highway, the man pulled over to the shoulder of the road, stopped and asked his family, "How much money do you have?" Their pooled resources came to a little under $100. He turned around and drove back to where the couple was still walking. "Do you still have the $20 bill I gave you?" he asked.

Quite surprised, the woman said, "Of course."

"Then give it back to me," he said.

Perplexed, she reached into her pocket and pulled out the $20 and handed it back to him. He then combined it with the money his family had pooled and handed it all to her saying, "Here, our family would like you to have this."

The first time I heard this story I was touched by it. On further contemplation I thought what a beautiful illustration of how God treats us. We are on the receiving end of so many great and wonderful gifts. Every day is marked by the gifts we receive. But at some point He comes to us and in so many words says, "Give them all back to Me, yes, all of them." Why? He does this so that He can combine them with His unlimited resources so they can be given to others. In reality, we own nothing. Everything we have is on loan to us for a short period of time. They were His before we came along, and they will be transferred to someone else upon our death. We brought nothing into this world, and we will take nothing out. But there is one way to "keep" it—it's when we give it away! Even a cup of cold water which is given in His name will eventually produce a reward. In an act of unselfish giving, we tap into the infinite resources of God!

Some anonymous banking officer calculated that if the widow's "mite" in Jesus' day had been deposited in the "First National Bank of Jerusalem" to draw 4% interest semi-annually, the fund today would total approximately $4,800,000,000,000,000,000,000! What kind of interest do you suppose that gift has been drawing in the bank of heaven?

Generous people forget what they have given but gratefully remember what they have received. We have been reminded that if we have freely received something, we in turn should also freely give it.

(Mark 12:43; Matthew 10:8)

 POWER POINT: What have you been recently given that you could pass on to another?

Chapter 13

WHAT MADE HIM GIVE IT?

Here is an old story that comes to us from the Near East:

A monk who was traveling by foot in the mountains found a precious stone in a clear stream. The next day he met another traveler who was hungry, so the monk opened his knapsack to share his food.

The hungry traveler saw the precious stone in the monk's bag, asked to see it, admired it, and boldly asked the monk to give it to him. To his astonishment, the monk handed it over without hesitation.

The traveler left, happy and rejoicing in his good fortune. He knew the jewel was worth enough to provide him with financial security for the rest of his life. But he couldn't stop thinking about the monk. A few days later, he returned to the path he had traveled searching for the monk.

When he found him, he returned the precious stone and said, "I have been thinking. I know how valuable this stone is and that you also knew it to be valuable. But I give it back to you in the hope that you can give me something more precious than this jewel. If you can, let me have whatever it is that enabled you to freely give me this stone."

What is more valuable than an uncut precious stone? The attitude of unselfish giving...the inner something that allows you to give without asking for anything in return...the right stuff to give so another can be benefited...these are beyond all price.

When it comes to giving and living, too many of us are like the woman who excitedly told her friends about a Red Cross first-aid class which she had just completed: "Just yesterday, I was driving down 45th Street and sitting at a stop sign when I heard this awful crash behind me. I pulled my car to the side of the street and ran back to discover a car wrapped around a telephone pole. When I got to the injured driver, it was just terrible...blood was everywhere. My knees went limp, and I didn't know what to do. But all at once I remembered something from my first-aid training class. Immediately I sat down on the curb and bent over and put my head between my knees and it worked. I didn't even faint."

Sad...but too true. She was trained all right, but she had forgotten the real purpose of her training—to help others when the need arose. Too many of us forget that we have become Christians so that we can give! And help! And encourage! And give some more!

What makes a person become a "giver"? What happens on the inside in order to turn a selfish, self-centered, look-out-for-number-one kind of person into someone who gives? What is that inner quality which allows a person to freely give up something that is precious so another can receive the benefit?

There's a major clue to that in the following story. The man was wealthy and curious, someone who had an intense desire to see a celebrity who was traveling through town. Maybe you remember singing songs about this wealthy man in Sunday School as a child. "Zacchaeus was a wee little man and a wee little man was he, he climbed up in a sycamore tree the Savior for to see…"

What changed him? What caused Zacchaeus to be more than willing to give half of all he possessed to the poor and promise to pay back four times the amount to all whom he had cheated? An encounter with Jesus Christ! You can read the entire biblical account in Luke 19:1-10. But the conclusion is important. Jesus said to him, "Today salvation has come to this house, because this man, too, is a son of Abraham. For the Son of Man came to seek and to save what was lost" (Luke 19:9-10). How do we know there was a change of heart in this man? By his actions! By his attitude! By his generosity! Immediately after the encounter, he said, "Look, Lord! Here and now I give half of my possessions to the poor…" (Luke 19:8a) How long did it take to change this man? Not long!

If you're one of those people struggling with a selfish heart toward the needs of others, you need a personal encounter with Jesus Christ! There's an Old Testament promise that if people will turn to Him,

God says, "I will remove from them their heart of stone and give them a heart of flesh. Then they will follow my decrees and be careful to keep my laws. They will be my people, and I will be their God" (Ezekiel 11:19b-20).

What makes a person a giver? There's a simple and short answer—the change of heart which comes through an encounter with the God who can change any hard heart into a caring one!

(Luke 19:1-10; Ezekiel 11:19-20)

⚡ POWER POINT: Do you need a more caring heart? Turn to God and ask Him to help you and you may be amazed at the results.

Chapter 14

GRACEFUL GIVING

Grace was one of those simple, behind-the-scenes, quiet, typical "little-old-lady" types you find in most every church. She had never married and was now a retired school lunchroom employee who lived on a very meager, fixed income. Grace tithed (gave 10%) faithfully and consistently. But not only did she tithe, she went the second mile in her giving. Grace *always* gave $5 in honor of the memory of any church member who died. She *always* gave $2 to every special missions project or missionary who came our way. And she *always* supported the children and youth by baking her own special brand of cookies for their weekly meetings.

However, Grace's most important gifts to the church family were the birthday and anniversary cards she sent to every member. She overlooked no one, young or old. She had a notebook filled with their special dates and thoughtfully picked out a card that would fit each person. None of those "one style fits everyone" cards for her. Each was a special effort; each was different and distinctive. But they all had a common theme: they were the kind of cards I call "spirit-lifters."

When Grace's family was going through some of her things after she died, they found six months worth of birthday and anniversary cards already filled out with a handwritten message, addressed, and ready to be mailed. Each envelope had the mailing date penciled in where the stamp was to be placed. Her family honored Grace's love for people and her ministry of giving by mailing those prepared cards on the appropriate dates.

Why did Grace do this? Why would one who was probably least able to afford it, give so much? She gave out of her gratitude for God's love and forgiveness in her own life.

The only real motivation for giving that I can find comes out of compassion; it comes out of that personal encounter with Jesus Christ; it comes out of a transformed heart; it grows out of a heart that has been softened to the hurts and needs of others. Graceful giving! What a way to live! What a legacy to leave behind! What a memorial! What an encourager!

No matter how humble the circumstances of your lifestyle, you can still be a giver. Giving is not to be measured in the *amount* but in the *action*. If you can't give as much as others more fortunate, you can give what you have in an attitude of loving gracefulness. Take a look around you. Do you see a need? Then fill it in the best way you can. If all you have to give is an encouraging word, then give it! In today's cynical world, that's a precious commodity.

It's not in the size or quantity that the value of a gift is measured; the measurement is in the "heart" of the giver. The world's most famous giver is an anonymous widow and the most famous gift was a "mite" or two very small copper coins, and her story is worth reading once more: As he looked up, Jesus saw the rich putting their gifts into the temple treasury. He also saw a poor widow put in two very small copper coins. "I tell you the truth," He said, "this poor widow has put in more than all the others. All these people gave their gifts out of their wealth; but she, out of her poverty, put in all she had to live on" (Luke 21:1-4). What do you calculate will be her eternal reward? What will she be honored for in heaven?

Powerful givers and powerful gifts make a lasting impact, but it is felt even more by the giver than the recipient.

The next time you plan a gift, remember a "Graceful" giver and an anonymous widow...ladies who gave out of their poverty!

(Luke 21:1-4)

⚡ POWER POINT: Do you know someone who could benefit by a word of encouragement? Why not give them a call or write them a letter today!

Chapter 15

A PARABLE FROM THE BIRDS

Three young birds were desperately hanging onto a dead branch that stretched out over a lake. Their mother had just pushed them out of the nearby nest. Perched alongside the chicks, she began shoving them toward the end of the branch. Finally, the little bird on the end fell off. Something interesting happened about six feet below the branch—the little bird's wings started flapping, and it managed to fly over to the next tree.

Then the second little bird also fell, and it managed to fly away, too. But not the third one. This one was stubborn. It was determined not to be pushed off the branch because it had no faith that it could fly. This little chick held on for dear life. Its grip on the branch eventually loosened just enough so that its little body swung downward. Swiftly its talons tightened once more, and there it hung upside down, bulldog tenacious. No way was it about to let go, not ever, if it had its way.

But the parent bird had no sympathy for the stubborn little one. The mother immediately began pecking at the clutching talons. Soon it became more painful for the chick to hang on than it was to risk the uncertainty of flying. At last, the inevitable happened and the little bird began to fall. Suddenly its wings began pumping furiously, and it managed to fly up into the next tree with the others.

Why was the mother bird seemingly cruel to her fledgling? She knew what her baby didn't know—that it would be able to fly when it had to! Really, there was not one bit of danger in making the little one do what it was originally created to do!

When birds were created, their feet were made like claws or talons with which they can grasp a branch and hold on securely. But above all, birds were created to fly. Flying allows them to be at their best and most graceful. God created them to be flyers!

Giving is what we humans were designed to do best! This is what we were born to do, or more exactly, born-again to do! This is our purpose; it was carefully designed into us before we were born. As birds were created to fly, we have been created to give because we are made in God's image!

However, many of us will do anything necessary to live for ourselves and hold tightly to our possessions. That little bird looked pretty pathetic hanging upside down holding onto that bit of security. Likewise, we look pathetic clutching tightly the "branches" of our bank accounts, our brokerage accounts, our mutual funds, our annuities, our earthly possessions. We are scared to death to let go of them and fly on the untested wings of giving. We are afraid to live generously because we have never tried it!

Do you believe God speaks the truth? Come on, be honest! Do you believe God has been truthful with you when it comes to this aspect of giving? God is very specific in His Word. He will do all He can to shove you away from your securities in order to get you to soar on His promises. Try and read the following with an open mind:

> *Whoever sows [gives] sparingly will also reap sparingly, and whoever sows [gives] generously will also reap generously. Each…should give what he has decided in his heart to give, not reluctantly or under compulsion, for God loves a cheerful giver. And God is able to make all grace abound to you, so that in all things at all times, having all that you need, you will abound in every good work! Now he who supplies seed to the sower and bread for food will also supply and increase your store of seed and will enlarge the harvest of your righteousness! You will be made rich in every way so that you can be generous on every occasion and through us your generosity will result in thanksgiving to God* (2 Corinthians 9:6-8, 10-11).

Doesn't this promise from God strip away all the excuses that your selfish heart and soul come up with when confronted with an opportunity to be generous?

Believe this: THERE IS NO WAY THAT YOU CAN OUTGIVE GOD!

(2 Corinthians 9:6-8, 10-11)

⚡ POWER POINT: Let me challenge you to jump out of your nest and ask God for direction on how to give to a neighbor.

Chapter 16

THE ANONYMOUS GIVER

Are you fascinated by anonymous givers? I don't know about you, but I sure am. Perhaps you may have read this story which first appeared in *Time* magazine, on February 3, 1997. It's been commented on and written about in any number of editorials in newspapers and other publications. Yes, it really is true.

The anonymous giver's name is Charles Feeney, although he is no longer anonymous through no fault of his own. He made his fortune by owning and operating a large number of duty-free shops at airports, terminals, and border crossings. Secretly he has been giving his money away!

How was he uncovered? He finally was forced to confess to his good deeds when the company who bought his business sued him in order to find out what he did with all his earnings. They couldn't believe it was as lucrative as he said, so they brought a lawsuit against him and he was forced to confess it all.

Feeney has been one of the most generous and giving people this world has ever seen. How much did he give away anonymously? Hold on—he gave away $600 million over the past 15 years! You're reading this correctly—$600 mil! In addition, he has put away $3.5 billion into his charitable foundations so the money can be distributed later! That's right, $3.5 billion!

And the records of his company show he still wasn't what anyone would call poverty stricken. He kept a measly $5 million for himself! Put that into perspective, however. He kept for himself about 1/10th of 1% of what he gave away! Staggering! Yes, that is correct, 1/10th of 1% of what he has given away!

Why? This is interesting. What really motivates a giver like this? The *New York Times* asked him, and he replied: "I simply decided I had enough money."

Now, are you ready for this? Charles Feeney is a rich man...not because he has $5 million, but because he's decided, "I have enough!" He's like very few other people in this world. How many people do you know have said, "I have enough." Ask most people, rich or poor, if they have enough. If they are honest with you, they will likely say, "I need a little bit more."

Having enough has to be a major secret to living a successful life! When should we say *enough?* And when you have reached that level, what will you be doing with the amount that is over and above your own personal "enough"? Why, of course, give it away! Talk about being a positive example in a world gone money grubbing mad! Talk about a lifestyle that stands against all this world system seems to stand for...Charles Feeney understood the principle of "enough."

There is a powerful little message tucked away in the book of Proverbs which has been overlooked for too long. It's found in the prayer of a man named Agur: "Two things I ask of you, O Lord; do not refuse me before I die: Keep falsehood and lies far from me; give me neither poverty nor riches, but give me only my daily bread. Otherwise, I may have too much and disown you and say, 'Who is the Lord?' Or I may become poor and steal, and so dishonor the name of my God" (Proverbs 30:7-9).

Are you rich? Rich enough to say "enough"? What a powerful concept and what a powerful incentive to be a generous giver!

Before we leave this subject, there is one more thing we need to consider. Does the Bible have anything to say about being an "anonymous" giver? Read that answer with me:

> Be careful not to do your "acts of righteousness" before men, to be seen by them. If you do, you will have no reward from your Father in heaven. So when you give to the needy, do not announce it with trumpets, as the hypocrites do in the synagogues and on the streets, in order to be honored by men. I tell you the truth, they have received their reward in full. But when you give to the needy, do not let your left hand know what your right hand is doing, so that your giving may be in secret. Then your Father, who sees what is done in secret, will reward you (Matthew 6:1-4).

(Matthew 6:1-4; Proverbs 30:7-9)

⚡ POWER POINT: Try sending a gift to someone anonymously. Watch their reaction, but don't spill the beans!

Chapter 17

GIVING KINDNESS TO AN ENEMY

Eight times the Ministry of Education in former East Germany said "no" to Uwe Holmer's children when they had attempted to enroll at the University in East Berlin. The Ministry of Education wasn't in the business of giving out the reasons for its rejection of applicants for enrollment. However, in this case the reason was obvious—Uwe Holmer, the father of the applicants, was a Lutheran pastor at Lobetal, a suburb of East Berlin.

For a little more than 26 years, the Ministry of Education was headed by Margot Honecker, wife of East Germany's premier, Erich Honecker. But then the Berlin wall was smashed to the ground. Quickly, Honecker and his wife were unceremoniously ousted from their offices. He was indicted for criminal activities which he committed during his tenure as premier.

In the middle of a bitterly cold winter, the Honeckers were evicted from their luxurious palace in Vandlitz, an exclusive suburb which had been reserved for use by the VIPs in the Communist party.

The Honeckers were suddenly without friends, without any resources, stripped of their possessions, and with absolutely no place to go for shelter. Not a single one of their former cronies or government officials showed them a bit of the humanitarianism the Communists had proudly boasted about. No one wanted to be identified with the Honeckers. No one from their past offered them anything by way of help.

At this point enters Pastor Uwe Holmer who remembered the words of Jesus, "If someone strikes you on the right cheek, turn to him the other also" (Matthew 5:39). He didn't stop there, but continued, "You have heard that it was said, 'Love your neighbor and hate your enemy.' But I tell you: Love your enemies and pray for those who persecute you, that you may be sons of your Father in heaven" (Matthew 5:43-45a). That's heady stuff. Give your enemy the other cheek…give your enemy love…that you might be known as children of the heavenly Father!

So Pastor and Mrs. Holmer issued a gracious invitation to the Honeckers to move in with their family in the parsonage of the parish church in Lobetal!

According to an article by Joel C. Gerlach in *The Northwestern Lutheran*, "Pastor Holmer has not yet reported that the Honeckers have renounced their atheism and professed faith in Jesus as Savior and Lord. But at least they fold their hands and bow their heads when the family prays together!"

Incredible! What an extraordinary story. Who knows, other than God, what will eventually happen in the lives of the Honeckers? Who knows what kind of actions have been triggered in the Holmer's parishioners by the kind of love they watched their pastor and his family give so freely?

Contrary to the world's wisdom, what does the Bible say that we are to give when faced with a lawsuit or when someone is trying to stiff arm you? "If someone wants to sue you and take your tunic, let him have your cloak as well. If someone forces you to go one mile, go with him two miles. Give to the one who asks you, and do not turn away from the one who wants to borrow from you" (Matthew 5:40-42).

Need I say more? Nothing other than...go and do likewise!

(Matthew 5:39-43)

⚡ POWER POINT: Do you know anyone who has come upon hard times—either financially or personally? Ask God to show you what you can do for them that will make a difference.

Chapter 18

IF I HAD MORE, I'D GIVE MORE

A man once said, "If I had some extra money, I'd give it to God, but I have just enough to support myself and my family." The same man also said, "If I had some extra time, I'd give it to God…but every minute is taken up with my job, my family, my clubs, and what-have-you, every single minute." He continued further, "If I had a talent, I'd give it to God, but I have no lovely voice; I have no special skill; I've never been able to lead a group; I can't think cleverly or quickly the way I would like to."

Has your excuse for not giving time, talent, or resources been: "I don't have anything to give…"? Stop right there. How can you or I, living in this land of abundance, living a lifestyle that is the envy of the world, living like kings and queens compared to our grandparents or those in emerging third world countries, say we have nothing to give? How? Are we that ungrateful? Even the poorest among us has something to give.

Let's take a look at this issue from another angle. Congressman Bob McQuen from Ohio is a committed Christian who spends most of his time in Washington, D.C. He tells this story about his brother who took his young son to McDonalds® for lunch. He bought hamburgers, fries, and drinks and put the food down between them on the table. They began to enjoy their lunch together, talking about guy things. Dad then reached across for a couple of fries when, much to his surprise, his son grabs his hand and pulls the fries away saying, "These are mine!" The man was now in a bit of shock because his son reacted so selfishly.

As he reflected on his boy and on this episode, he told himself the following: 1) My son doesn't have any idea that I am the source of those fries in spite of the fact that just about ten minutes ago, I bought them. 2) I have the power, being the dad, to reach over and take those fries away from him. 3) I can go back to the counter, lay down a $50 bill, and tell them to bury my son in fries. 4) I don't need his French fries, I can just as easily go back to that counter and buy all I want.

Then the thought struck him—God has provided us with all kinds of "fries" in life because He wants to share the blessings of life with us! When we refuse to share with God or others, He says, "Don't you understand I'm the source...I have the power...and I don't need your gifts because they are already mine?!" What a revelation!

God wants us to share and give, not because He's hurting and needs it, but because He has shown us how to give, and He wants it passed on to others.

One of the first Bible verses people usually memorize is John 3:16: "For God so loved the world that He gave His only begotten Son…" This was the greatest act of giving ever! But you can turn to almost any other page in your Bible, and you will see God in the act of giving.

The principle which needs to be understood is EVERYTHING COMES FROM GOD! EVERYTHING! King David understood this principle when he began gathering materials to build the temple. He prayed, "Everything in heaven and earth is Yours…Everything comes from You, and we have given You only what comes from Your hand. O Lord our God, as for all this abundance that we have provided for building you a temple for your Holy Name, it comes from your hand, and all of it belongs to you!" (I Chronicles 29:11b, 14b, 16)

That takes the wind out of the excuse, "if I had more I would gladly give it." Start your giving where you are with what you have already been given. The bottom line is that God will require nothing of us that He has not already given!

(John 3:16; I Chronicles 29:11b, 14b, 16)

 POWER POINT: See how many verses you can find in the Bible that talk about God's giving.

Chapter 19

LOSING AND FINDING

Marian Preminger was born in Hungary in 1913 and was raised in a castle with her aristocratic family. She was surrounded with maids, tutors, governesses, butlers, and chauffeurs. Her grandmother, who lived with them, insisted that whenever they traveled, they take their own linen because she believed it was beneath their dignity to sleep between sheets used by common people.

While attending school in Vienna, Marian met a handsome young Viennese doctor. They fell in love and eloped when she was only 18. The marriage only lasted a year, and she returned to Vienna to begin life as an actress.

While auditioning for a play, she met the brilliant young German director, Otto Preminger. They fell in love and soon married. They traveled to America where he began his career as a movie director. Tragically, Marian was caught up in the glamour, lights, and superficial excitement of Hollywood and soon began to live a sordid life. When Preminger discovered it, he divorced her.

Marian returned to Europe to live the life of a socialite in Paris. In 1948, she learned from the newspaper that Albert Schweitzer, a man she had read about as a little girl, was making one of his periodic visits to Europe and was staying at Gunsbach. She phoned his secretary and was given an appointment to see Dr. Schweitzer the next day. When Marian arrived in Gunsbach, she found him in the village church playing beautiful organ music. After visiting with her, he invited Marian to have dinner at his house. By the end of the evening, she knew she had discovered what she had been looking for all her life. When he returned to Africa, he invited her to come to Lambarene and work in the hospital.

Marian did, and began for the first time to give herself in service to others. There in Lambarene, the girl who was born in a castle and raised like a princess, who was accustomed to being waited on with all the luxuries of a spoiled life, became a servant! A giver! She changed bandages, bathed babies, fed lepers...and set herself free.

Marian later wrote her autobiography and called it *All I Ever Wanted Was Everything*. She stated she could not get the "everything" which would satisfy her and give meaning to her life until she could gave everything. When she died in 1979, the New York Times carried her obituary which included this statement from her: "Albert Schweitzer said there are two classes of people in this world...the helpers and the non-helpers. I'm a helper." Being a helper means being a giver!

As she gave herself away, she found herself. It's in giving that we really find ourselves. Are you still searching for yourself? Dissatisfied with your lifestyle? Unfulfilled in what you are doing? The action of giving could change all that very quickly.

Okay...so when do you begin changing? In Lewis Thomas' autobiography, *The Youngest Science: Notes of a Medicine Watcher* (Viking 1983), he shares the following story.

While working as a resident in a Boston Hospital, Thomas learned of an interesting case. That morning, a young musician, who had experienced chills and fever during the previous week, was admitted to the hospital in bad shape. The patient's blood samples revealed malaria, a disease so unusual in Boston that many on the staff took specimens for further study.

As the day wore on, a growing number of physicians and medical students came to the patient's bedside to observe this remarkable case for themselves. But all this interest didn't help the patient. The young man became increasingly drowsy as clumps of infected cells blocked more and more of his brain's blood vessels. He lapsed into a coma and by evening he was dead.

Silently, the hospital medical director left the group standing around the bed and returned with a copy of the medical textbook he had fetched from his office. Opening it to the chapter on malaria, he read the following passage to his assembled colleagues: "Any doctor who allows a case of malaria to die without quinine is guilty of malpractice."

The young musician, who was an admitted heroin addict, had apparently shared a needle with an infected visitor from a tropical climate. While the treatment of malaria had long been part of medical training, none of the attending doctors did more than study the problem...until it was too late!

Don't you think it's time to get into action with a giving lifestyle? By waiting, someone may be placed in jeopardy. By waiting, we are postponing the flow of blessings to others as well as those that return to us. By waiting, nothing happens! Today is the day of action!

(Proverbs 12:25)

⚡ POWER POINT: Begin today by giving a kind word to someone in your family. We all must start somewhere! Then make a list of others with whom you might share a blessing.

Chapter 20

CASTING YOUR BREAD

Winston Churchill, as a boy, was visiting friends on an estate in Scotland. While swimming, he got cramps and began to drown. Alexander Fleming, who was about his same age and the son of the estate's gardener, saw him struggling, jumped in, and saved his life. Churchill's father was so thankful that he went to the boy's father, the gardener, and said, "Is there anything that I can do for you or your son to express my gratitude? Please tell me."

Alexander had a boyhood dream of becoming a medical doctor and specializing in research. This was an impossible dream considering the humble home in which he lived and the modest salary paid to his father. Mr. Fleming replied, "Mr. Churchill, my son desperately wants to go to medical school, and I simply can't afford to send him."

Winston Churchill's father immediately promised to send the young man all the way through medical school. He did, and Alexander graduated with honors.

Years passed...and Alexander Fleming became

known as one of the leading research doctors in the country. In the meantime, Winston had become Prime Minister. While Churchill was on a diplomatic mission to Egypt, he contracted pneumonia. The medical team attending him had given up hope that he would survive. Word was sent back to England. Was there any possible cure? Dr. Fleming was contacted and personally flew to Egypt with vials of his newest discovery in order to treat the Prime Minister. Yes, the Prime Minister recovered quite quickly with the miracle cure that Dr. Alexander Fleming had discovered—penicillin! Alexander not only saved the lives of countless people around the world, he also saved the life of Winston Churchill for a second time!

How do you know what will happen because of a gift you give? How your gift is used is none of your business, but when you unselfishly give, you trigger into action one of those special laws of the universe. You will not only reap what you sow, you will reap *more than* you sow.

The wisest man who ever lived penned these lines: "Cast your bread upon the waters, for after many days you will find it again" (Ecclesiastes 11:1). We are not to give, expecting the same kind of gift in turn, or it's not really a gift. When you count on a return, it's really just an investment. But whatever you truly give as a *gift* sets into motion a powerful return!

Orvil Reid was a busy missionary when 12-year-old Jose Gonzalez came into his life. Jose had come to Guadalajara to find work. At night, he slept in the ovens of a bakery after they had cooled. He was dirty, unkempt, underfoot, full of questions, and a nuisance.

Reid invited Jose to live in the student house he had opened as a ministry for orphaned children and to attend school with them. The boy also began to work in a print shop. He was a quick learner and eventually graduated from medical school at the University of Guadalajara and became a leading internist and cardiologist. For a time, Dr. Gonzalez was chief resident at Methodist Hospital in Dallas, Texas.

Orvil retired from missionary work and moved to Dallas. Quite suddenly one evening, he suffered a severe heart attack. When Reid's wife called their family doctor, to her surprise, Dr. Gonzalez, who happened to be visiting, answered the phone. The two doctors immediately had the retired missionary rushed to the hospital emergency room where Dr. Gonzalez did open heart surgery to remove the blockages which caused the heart attack. He was the only doctor available who had the necessary training and experience at the time to perform the delicate operation. And missionary Orvil Reid recovered quite nicely.

Think about it...the man who had extended a helping hand to Jose—a simple beggar lad in need—had a surgeon's skillful hand given back to him! Does it work like that all the time? Maybe not quite as dramatically, but it always works! Whatever is planted will eventually produce a harvest. That's a law that is written in the universe. Let's harness it for good!

⚡ POWER POINT: What kind of bread can you cast upon the waters this week? Record your experiences in a notebook and read it over after one year. You probably will be surprised what has happened.

Chapter 21

ARE YOU A "GIMPER GIVER"?

What do the whooping crane, the cheetah, the black rhino, the California condor, the buffalo, and the "gimper" have in common?

They are all rare. Not extinct—just rare. The first five are rare because our civilization has been destroying their habitat. "Gimpers" are rare because our society has not been developing them.

Okay, so what is a "gimper"? Never heard of the word? I hadn't either until I was in the audience of a motivational speaker who talked about them. A "gimper" is someone who is determined to do their best regardless of the cost, one who strives for excellence in life. Now, do you see why I classified a gimper as being rare, not extinct, but rare? How many people could you identify as being a gimper?

Dan Betzer, a pastor, tells an interesting story. The phone rang in his office. A lady was calling to say she had heard the church needed a new piano. "We have a pretty good old one in our home," she began, "and we've just purchased a new one."

When I heard the story, I thought I knew what was coming next. I was sure Betzer would say, "And she said the church could have their old piano."

But that wasn't the case. She went on, "We want the church to have the new one. We can get along with our old one just fine, but God's church should have the best!"

There goes another gimper! God doesn't want our leftovers or used stuff. God and His people are not a goodwill box. God wants and expects our best when we give to Him, His Church, or any of His people.

One day a gimper met Jesus. It was at a supper given in His honor. Apparently the celebration was by invitation only, but somehow this gimper made her way to Jesus. Their eyes met. Then she took a flask of precious spikenard, broke off the neck, and poured the contents on Christ's head. Immediately her action was criticized by the other guests, "What a waste!" "Too extravagant!" "It should have been sold and given to the poor!" "Foolish!"

But Jesus thought differently. "Leave her alone," said Jesus. "Why are you bothering her? She has done a beautiful thing to me" (Mark 14:6a). The Master so prized her gift that He said wherever and whenever the Gospel would be preached, what she had given would be an eternal memorial to her. She meets the qualifications of being a blue ribbon gimper. A special woman among women. Why?

Her gift was *unannounced*. Did she have an engraved invitation? No! Nowhere is there any kind of hint that someone asked her to perform the generous deed. She saw a need and knew she had the ability to meet it, so she did!

Her gift was prized because she was *motivated by love*! It's important that the people of God be led by the Spirit of God and not by any selfish reasons. She did not expect to receive any recognition for her action. She simply responded to his ministry with love.

Her gift was prized because she gave *her best*. The alabaster jar of spikenard was a costly spice imported from India. In Mark's account he informs us that it was worth more than a year's wages! She gave her best!

She was praised because she did what she could *before it was too late*. Mark 14:1 tells us that this banquet was only two days before the Passover—in other words, just two short days before the crucifixion of Jesus Christ. The guests around the table must have been thinking, "This woman is a fool. Jesus is only 33 years old. He's going to be with us for a long time to come."

What would have happened had she decided it would be a foolish act to buy the spikenard? She would have missed the once in a lifetime opportunity to anoint His body beforehand for burial. Jesus said so. Just a few short days later, He was dead! She did what she could before it was too late!

As a minister I have stood with family members at open graves and heard them—a spouse, a son, a daughter, a relative, a friend—say through tears of remorse, "If only I had…"

Don't put off your gift giving! Step up, get into action, become another "GIMPER"! Do your best for God, for His people, for His Church, and for others before it's too late!

(Mark 14:1-9)

⚡ POWER POINT: Is there something you have been putting off doing for someone? Do it before it's too late!

Chapter 22

A GOOD WORD FOR SANTA

No book on the power of gift giving would be complete, at least in my humble opinion, without at least one Christmas story. So let's start with jolly old St. Nick, himself.

Nicolas was born of wealthy parents in A.D. 280 in a small town called Patara in Asia Minor. He lost his parents early in life through an epidemic but not before they had instilled in him the gift of faith and generosity. Little Nicolas went to Myra and lived a life which was marked by sacrifice, love, and the spirit of Jesus Christ. Nicolas' life became so Christ-like that in later years he was asked to be bishop of the town.

There have been many stories of his generosity and compassion: how he begged for food for the poor and how he gave money to young girls so they would have a dowry, which was necessary in those days for them to get married. The story most often told is how he put on a disguise and went into the town to give gifts to poor children. He literally gave away everything he had inherited. Especially on Christmas Eve, he would put on his disguise and leave presents on the doorsteps of the poor families in his area.

But this simple story of St. Nicolas didn't die with him, it has spread around the world. Did you know that there are more churches in the world named in his honor than any other person in the history of the church?

Yes, I know, people have done strange things to him. The poet, Clement Moore, gave him a sleigh and eight tiny reindeer. Thomas Nast, the illustrator, made him big and fat and painted him in a red suit trimmed in white fur. Others have given him names... Belsnickle, Kris Kringle, Santa Claus. But what is really important about him is that he had the mind of Christ and lived a life of selfless love. He touched the whole world with the generosity which marked his life. And my prayer is that all of us would model our life after the man who followed the Man who gave us the greatest gift of all.

Christmas, in reality, is a celebration of giving! But, unfortunately in today's world, it's so easy to forget why we celebrate Christmas. We need to follow the example of Nicolas and make it a yearlong lifestyle of giving.

When God wants something important accomplished in this world, He does it differently than we would. If we had his power, we would loose thunderbolts, shake the earth with a quake, darken the sun, blow up volcanoes, do anything that is noisy and dramatic. Not God. He simply sent a tiny, helpless baby, born in an obscure out-of-the-way place, and gave that baby a humble family.

Our gift giving is most powerful when done *in His way, with His attitude, and in His timing.* How much does God want to accomplish in His world through your generosity? Your kindness? Your willingness to give? And through your gifts?

And finally...

YOU CAN GIVE WITHOUT LOVING, BUT YOU CAN'T LOVE WITHOUT GIVING! This world will not care one whit about what we know, until they know that we care!

Love is the key to meaningful gift giving!

(John 3:16; Mark 12:31-33)

 POWER POINT: This Christmas participate in an angel tree project in your town.

Chapter 23

THE JOY OF GIVING

As a minister, I have invested 40 years of my life asking people to give. I have received approximately 6,240 offerings and been part of raising millions of dollars for the church and the church family, as well as for a myriad of missionaries, college building programs, camping programs, etc. A good portion of my life has been spent helping people learn the joy of giving. There are some observations which have naturally become evident over these years. One fact, however, stands head and shoulders above all the others: The happiest people on the face of this earth are those who have learned the joy of giving!

I've observed people who've given on a regular basis week after week and have seen how they have matured through the process of giving. I have been privileged to watch drastic transformations of behavior take place. It has been a most exciting journey. I've watched hundreds of people experience joy in hundreds of different situations.

I saw joy in the face of Margaret, a little old lady who decided to take on a Saturday housecleaning job so that she could give $5 per week to the church building program.

I saw it eventually in the face of Bill, a retired railroad man, who was originally one of the most stingy men I'd ever met. He could squeeze old Abe until he yelled for relief. Then I watched as he committed his life to God and promised he would become a giver! He worked as a handyman doing odd jobs. He told me with tears in his eyes, "God has blessed so much after I learned how to give in my retirement years. He has given me more work than I can handle. In fact, Pastor, I made more money this past year than in any year during my working career with the railroad."

I heard it in the voice of a businessman, Frank, who made a commitment to give a million dollar gift so that his church could build a new sanctuary. Later he filed for bankruptcy but told me that nothing he had done in his life meant as much to him as that gift. He had no regrets, now that he was broke, or that he had given away a million. In fact, he said, "The only thing I still have is what I have given away!"

I felt the emotions of a young couple, David and Juanita, when they came to tell me they were postponing building their new home. They decided to give the money they saved for their dream home so a new church could be built in Africa.

I was amazed at the sacrificial gift of diamond wedding rings which were placed in the offering plate by Bev as we received an offering so land could be purchased for a new church. Later she said, "I wanted to give something that really represented me. I have no regrets. I have never felt so wonderful."

I saw the sparkle in the eyes of a twelve-year-old girl, Janette, who babysat, mowed lawns, saved her pennies, didn't buy sodas at noon, and refused to spend anything at McDonalds for more than six months so she could bring her $50 dollar gift for a needy children's home in Mexico. She later sold cookies to raise another $100 for the same cause. Why? She said, "The joy felt so good I wanted to do it again."

I observed the glow of pride in the eyes of a retired couple, Paul and Fran, who had saved money for a new car. But when they purchased the car, they brought the keys to me so I could give them to a missionary in the states whose car had worn out.

I've watched tears flow freely from the eyes of an entire congregation who for weeks had prepared their special offerings of love for six different home missions pastors. These pastors served in very small out of the way places, places nobody seemed to want to serve, and they've done so at great personal sacrifice. During our special "Home Missions Christmas" celebration, the congregation presented an abundant grocery shower, money, gifts for everyone from the youngest to the oldest, new suits, new shoes—all prepared and given with love.

Here is a final observation from all these years and all these experiences: Never once, that's right, *not once*, did I ever hear anyone say they regretted their sacrifices! And almost to a person, they also said they wished they had come to know the joy of giving long before they discovered it!

Here it is one more time: THE HAPPIEST PEOPLE I KNOW LIVING ON THE FACE OF THIS EARTH ARE THE PEOPLE WHO KNOW HOW TO GIVE!!

Other books by Robert Strand
in the Power Book series:

The Power of Forgiving
Never-to-be-forgotten stories and teaching that vividly depict and teach the concept of forgiving others as something that is intrinsic to our peace and joy.
ISBN 1-58169-050-9 96 pg. PB $5.95

The Power of Thanksgiving
Stories and teaching that demonstrate the difference that a lifestyle of thanksgiving can make in our lives.
ISBN 1-58169-054-1 96 pg. PB $5.95

Other pocket-sized books
from Evergreen Press:

The Little Book of Business Wisdom by Brian Banashak
Business wisdom for the novice and veteran alike. Packed with 88 principles for success—each with Scripture verse and testimony.
ISBN 1-58169-041-X 96 pg. PB $5.95

Proverbs of Success by John Grogan
The heart and soul of highly effective people. John Grogan has been a professional trainer and speaker for over 30 years. This book captures the essence of the wisdom he has shared with audiences around the globe.
ISBN 1-58169-045-2 96 pg. PB $5.95